WHEN
LOVE
RISES

ISBN-10: 978-0-9855527-2-5
ISBN-13: 978-0-9855527-3-2 (ebook)

Cover Design by Mark Hobbs
Illustrations by Anna Valenty

This book is a work of fiction. Names, characters, places, and events are the product of the author's imagination or are used factiously. Any resemblance to actual events or locales or persons, living or deceased, is coincidental.

WHEN
LOVE
RISES

Michelle G. Stradford

Poetic Reflections & Prose On
Loving, Hurting & Letting Go

Also By Michelle G. Stradford

I'm Rising: Determined. Confident. Powerful

DEAR READER

Thank you for reading my book. These words and thoughts were not always easily captured. Some arrived in free-flowing joyous moments, treasured memories that leaped onto the page. Others, at times, painfully extracted through an emotional tear letting process of meditational self-reflection, regret, harsh recrimination, murky memory diving, and uncomfortable self-awareness. But it was all so worth the effort to birth the prose that may somehow resonate with you, evoke an emotion or create a connection. I hope that you find meaning, and a shared experience in this first collection of my "Rising" series, expressing my interpretation of the exquisite emotion we call Love.

I have always been fascinated with hummingbirds, so you will see them represented in images throughout this book. In Native American culture, they are treasured as healers and harbingers of love, good luck, and joy. In other parts of the world, they are a sign of love, with the promise to bring it to the person who sees them.

DEDICATION

This book is dedicated to my mother, Virginia. Known as everyone's mom, she has a way of making all who know her feel genuinely loved and cared for. Thank you for teaching me how to love and that inviting others into our hearts expand what we are capable of.

TABLE OF CONTENTS

*Use your special
ingredients to
create your own happy*

LOVE RISING

LOVE RISING

I

Shine

like ten billion suns

when I'm in

your orbit.

| **Ten Billion Suns**

My rambling heart
find refuge
inside your
cavernous vessel.
I fill you.
You still me.

| *Soulmate*

I feel you in delicate
fragments
as you slowly reveal
your hand of hearts.
Those rapid
hummingbird movements
flutter in and out
of my life
playful and fleeting,
teasing up my emotions,
cautioning me
that you may never be
held captive.
I smile and coax away
a colorful feather
when you wisp by.
This essence of you
I will covet
until you return
and reveal the reason
you keep humming
my song.

| **Fragments**

Is this
tremor in my voice,
vibration in my chest,
the anticipation
or the aftermath
of the sensation
of you?

| **Tremors**

I jumped without
a parachute
into this free fall.
A frantic ride,
spinning and gasping
for air
in the thrill,
aiming straight for you.
Please be there
when I land.

| *Trust Fall*

When I'm with you,
I teeter along
the edge of the
thin contradiction
of an imagined us,
struggling to master
the delicate art
of composure
high atop this
emotional tightrope,
wholly committed
to indifference
while desperately
wanting to fall.

| **Tightrope**

You found me
and my love
in the wildest state.
Pure and purposeful.
Provide what I want.
Take only what you need.
Then leave me to run free
and non-conflicted
like ocean waves lapping
at the pull of the moonlight,
content to just be.
No earthly heartbeat
will ever
tame me.

| **Pure Wild**

I see the tiny flame
flickering behind
your cool gaze.
I stir you.

| *Sparks*

After you spoke
I swallowed up
your sumptuous verses,
then my head swooned
to the music
in your rhythm.
And this poetry
you poured into my glass
took to me too fast,
words so thickly sweetened,
they cling to my vocals
silencing my voice.
Yet, I savor the taste
of this unlikely story,
a spicy serving
of romance
spontaneously
mixed up
to woo me.

| **Taste Poetic**

I wait
for him
on the chaise
as he sits
at the piano
and plays
out his thoughts
in melodic keys
coaxing the tension
down from my shoulders.
I turn and watch
it exit the room
leaving behind
it's raw emotion
to help me orchestrate
our latest battle to clear the air.
Instead of engaging me in talking it out
he lifts his finger to shush,
continuing to play
with one hand
while caressing my neck
with the other
gently kneading out
our discord,
strumming
my chords
in soothing
order.

Notes rise
and fall
on my lips
quieting and
tamping down
the voice
of the frustrated emotion
that moments before
awaited there
poised for an epic fight.
Instead
he lifts me high
on a crescendo
lit with candles
warmed by the heat
of the fire crackling
in the corner
until we both discover our why
that despite our battles
we have profound love
for each other.
And I remember how
he and his piano
tag teams
every time
to play me.

| **Piano Played**

Each day
apart from you
I hold fast
to the strength in your arms,
to the promises
we pledged,
to the future version
of a fearless us.

| *Future*

I spiral down these
unhinged emotions
frantically grabbing
hold of a few thin
traces of you
as I brace
for the
fall.

| **Love Unhinged**

You are the
rhyme in my day,
rhythm in my stride.
Yes, you are
my reason,
my art,
my ride or die.
Every night I hope
and I pray
to feel your pulse,
hear your melody
right now, and always
tapping in my heart,
lulling me into dreams.
You forever
here to stay,
waking me to love,
keeping me woke
to life this way.

| **Rhyme of Life**

I

touch

your skin,

just to feel

high heat surging

below your

surface.

| *Turbulence*

Endless nights
Wide and boundless
Seep into my
dark colorless recesses
Haunting me
In the wake
of the brilliant morning
Abandoned by reason
Stripped of will
Paralyzed
I move through time
Pierced and broken
Like a bleeding memory
Held fast
To flames leaping long
wild and mindless
A prisoner
to the blissful burn
Of your fire
Blue and raging

| **Blue Fire**

These

Aftershocks

Of You

Continue

To

Still Me.

| *After*

Your
colors
drown me
in fluid waves
thrashing up
wild white foam
casting crimson hues
of fluster across my face
revealing my private
thoughts
and the effect of your
rising tide
raising expectations
pulling me under
then lifting me up
on your high

| **Fluid**

I hide
behind this
sassy smile
so, you don't
catch me
falling for
you.

| **Please Catch Me**

The heat from
the blaze in your eyes
is stoking my embers
lighting the path to
my carefully constructed
will of steel;
keeper of my secrets,
protector of unwieldy passion.
It ignites old fuses
and races up
this fresh wall of fear
leaping higher,
growing stronger,
revealing this now
pliable and
molten heart.
You radiate.

| **Radiate**

Strung tight
on your
Spanish guitar,
you strum me
one kiss closer
to recklessness.
Just play me faster.
End this
breathless
note.

| *Spanish Guitar*

You surprise me.
Leaving me in wonder
that you're
gutsy enough
to return.
Yes, rise to love
an even wilder
more guarded me
for a second turn.

| **Seconds**

That luminous smile
Is slowing me down
It's making me wait
Making me brake
For you.
This glare
From your shine
It's holding me back.
Your love is
Blinding me.
I steal a look your way
Only to run a wreck
Stall out
And spin in place.
All caused by your
High and dangerous
Sun delay.

| **Sun Delay**

These
hushed whispers
undo me,
releases my
grounding to gravity.
With you, I soar,
dare to be free
Just let go.
Come fly with me.

| **When We Fly**

Unable to match
your stare
I search for a way out,
a door through which
to escape this dare.
My heart falters,
tripping over
the curve of your lips.
Steadied, I turn to leave
but those predator eyes
pierce me,
pinning me down,
ensnaring us inside of
this risky desire.

| **Ensnared**

I catch your glance
across the room
and read you
as those unveiled eyes
reveal the words
once disguised
by that perfectly
crooked smile.

No need to speak
your heart to me,
I feel it pulse
while in your arms.
Taste the wanton words
on your lips
each time I yield
to your charms.

I hear them in
your measured voice.
And those dancing
soulful eyes,
telegraph how
deep the well
that fuels your
smoldering desire.

They light this fire
inside of me.
Cast shine
beneath my smile.
Like raw current
jolts me back to life.
Yes, they make me
come alive.

When your voice
drifts across the room,
I hear your
inaudible words.
The ones you
dare not whisper
shout *You need me*
to me out loud.

| **Invisible Words**

Lulled
into a dream
faint with
imaginings of you
lurking at the edge
of my consciousness.
We dance to salty music
sashaying through the night
on enflamed souls,
you wanting more than
I am capable of.
Spellbound I consider
whether my life is
fertile enough to grow
a raw and rare love.
Then morning breaks
and there you are again
in my head like a lyric
that just won't end.

| **Dream Lyric**

Sometimes
I get lost in
your details
and marinate
inside of them
until I'm tender
enough to be
consumed.

| *Consumed*

Your luminous eyes
light up my dark
showing me all
I could not see.
They circle and pull me
back to you,
so strong and intense
it frightens me.

That piercing look,
it owns me.
Musing dancing eyes,
you're reading me.
Each thought of mine,
this dark abyss
inside of me
beneath the scars
only you can see.

I attempt, but fail
to turn away.
I'm riveted in place
by your gaze.
You captivate me.

Yes, your light
is just for me,
all about me,
you're needing me.
Though I try to escape,
to hide,
can't tear away
from those eyes.
You mesmerize.

| **Mesmerize**

His every phrase
wielded
all-pervading power
to lay me bare.

| ***Left Bare***

A hearty laugh
over shared sarcasm.
A raised eyebrow
met with nervous
wry attempted jokes.
The twenty-second
silent gaze.
When you finished
my artsy sentence
for the seventh time,
I knew you were
the only pickup line
I'd ever heed.

| **Pick Up Artist**

His eyes glisten
like freshly steamed
brown cacao beans
caught in the low
and translucent
golden sunbeams.
The moisture escaping
his sienna skin
vaporize my worries,
loosening the knots in
my shoulders.
Under the cerulean skies
that paint the coral key,
I rewrite the agenda
for my once
carefully scripted
day by the sea.

| **Cacao Cay**

I'm committed
only to me, I said.
You listened to
mountains of rants
and waded through
years of friend zone waters
until I was confident
enough to trust myself
to jump back into
the deep end.

| **Deep Patience**

Each day I arise
I promise to win
your hundred-watt smile
that knowing grin
Yes, recapture your heart
over and over again

| **Lasting Love**

I sprawl out wide
beneath our
favorite live oak
and open my mind
just long enough
to capture
a fleeting thought
as it flutters
on the edge of dusk
like the fireflies
we once captured
for just us
to glow inside
our mason jars.
I grab hold of the end
of a remembrance
gingerly
like the way
you would wisp
a stray curl
from my eyes.

I relive the
sunlit golden scenes
as they unfold and fuse
gone yesterdays
with future todays
and send me wondering
whether they were real
or imagined.
My eyelids swing open
pulling back the rosy glass
as I peer into the window
of my youth and see us
rolling in the grass,
beneath the scorching
Summer sun
and know that
we were real.

| **Summer**

I heard
your supposed
indifferent sarcasm
when I strode past you.
I shot back a quick response
so, you labeled
me saucy.

| *Saucy*

You bounded back
into the room
with a blazing smile
drying the mist
from my eyes,
thawing the frost
yet another fight
had glazed over
our indelible love.

| **Make Up**

The calm in your voice
silences my stormy unease,
reassures me that
no challenge is too great
for our duo, restoring
my faith in us.
You still me.

The fire in your eyes
lights up my dark places,
puts the warm in my chill,
yes, you torched all my walls,
imploding them with chemistry.
You excite me.

The sun in your laugh
strings my head and heart along
keeps my smile lit up in lights
making the days, ah…the nights
worth waiting and rising for.
You inspire me.

| **You Get Me**

You stroked

my fertile awakening

and cloaked me inside of

your protective loins

until we adjoined

then divided

infinitely into a life.

| **Conception**

I stumbled over
your energy zone
while rambling through
my head alone.
I smiled.
And treasure even more
the gift of you
as my one.

| *My One*

You care enough
to need to know
where I am,
and what I'm thinking.
Yes, your knowing
what I am doing,
ensuring that
I am okay
is incredibly freeing.
You taught the still
evolving me
that the right
balance of care
is neither controlling
or smothering,
but takes a
special touch of loving.
A hard-learned lesson
I surely needed
to know.

| **Need to Know**

The heat

rising from your skin

burned through

my veiled

resistance.

| Torched

Come live with me
in the twi-life,
amid purple misted stars
and hold on tight
while our hearts
race the night
into the bliss
of a powdered blue day.
We'll close the
blackout blinds
and push away
the gray day moon,
stealing intimate moments
that belong to the dark,
until twilight arrives,
beckoning us to race up
white euphoric peaks,
where we'll kiss
long and slow
in our golden afterglow,
beneath the velvet night
until love rises us
once more.

| **Live in Twi-Life**

I

Love You

With All This

Urgency

To Prevent

Tiny Fractures

From

Breaking

Through

| *Obsession*

Yes, you stimulate
my intellect,
stoke all my senses
with high discussion,
questions,
and charged debate.
You stir my attraction with
your sensitivity,
a stroke on my nape.
But before
I can open my heart
or allow you in my bed,
connect first with my mind.
Take a little more time
to get to know the me
that thrives
inside my head.

| **Mind play**

There is not much
sexier than one
exuding quiet confidence,
owning a
commanding presence,
wielding quick wit,
and staying humble
in their attractiveness.
Everyone has
a private definition
that moves them.
You embody mine.

| **Embody**

First
there is
Me
perhaps a
We
drifting
in and out
of my reverie.
Defying all effort
to push them away.
These incessant thoughts
keep making me feel
some kind of way.
Despite this thing
we say we're not in,
I stare down the clock
to lock in when
we can be there
for each other again.

| **Maybe We**

Liquid memories
of the newly us
ripple over our bodies
leaving ribbons of
red and golden sunsets
tattooed across
our love
kissed
skin

| **Maui Memoir**

Can you feel
my heart dancing
to the music
of our magic
factor?

| *Love's Dance*

I look hard at the memory
staring it down
willing it to stay
in the past where it belongs
Yet it will not be contained
Sliding off the glossy face
of the worn postcard
it comes to life
before me

I close my eyes to
escape
but am captivated
by colorful images
of days past
of moments lost
of him
I see lush foliage
laden with moisture
I hear water falling
crashing
onto smooth rocks
I open my eyes
and try to tear away
from the memory
unwilling to go back there
To the time when
I lost myself

I struggle with
the memory a bit longer
My eyes flutter
and close in
surrender
I am on the island now
surrounded by
the boundless sea
So broad
so deep
and alive
Salty mist clings to my skin
as the beige wet sand
massages my soul
I linger in the moment
then follow the memory
to the place where
I left my heart

We walk along
the beach
at dusk
bantering and laughing
just being us
A warm breeze nuzzles
the hair at my nape
as I revel in his presence
My eyes wide in wonder
head alight and fingers a tingle
The sound of his voice
pulses through me
in melodic stereo

When the caress of his hand
tightens over mine
I stop and turn to see
the light of truth in his eyes
Expectation in mine burns
low and warm
as I tremble with emotion
feeling raw and exposed
At the joining of our lips
my heart catches fire
takes a leap
and freefalls
landing safe
and secure in his arms

You can never go back they say
That which is lost to time
can never be recaptured
All moments must pass
Yet today I sit here
frozen in place
toying with this relic
from days past
because it is all I have left
of then
of him
of whom I thought
I would be

I turn the postcard over
and slowly trace the loops
of the letters of his name
A deep longing rises up
and takes hold of me
I am surprised by its fullness
at its freshness
I want to see his face
to touch his skin
I need to feel my heart
leap again

I reach up
and wipe my eyes
tucking away the memory
once more
and will me back to now
I stand and put the postcard
back into the book
slamming it tight
I place it high and safe
upon the shelf
Then reflect upon
the choices I have made
and know that
they were good ones
at the time

I am a different person now
one who is propelled
along this journey
by a quest to stand on my own
Driven by fear of dependence
fear of hurt
fear of losing me
There is no place in my life now
for that ethereal thing
that once clouded my vision
stripping me of control
of focus
that rendered me vulnerable
because I believed
in fate
in him
in love

Now that I am wiser
stronger
content
the flame
has been quieted
burned out and spent
So I rise
and retrieve the book
snatch out the postcard
and rip it apart

But the memory
it lives on
Haunting my soul
questioning and challenging
and testing my resolve
It rambles and smolders
beneath my skin
threatening to ignite
into fire again

| **Epic**

Love thrives
when planted in trust.
Grows stronger
through selflessness.
Weakens and wilts
when starved.
Shrivels and dies
in betrayal.
Nurture it.

| *Love Thrives*

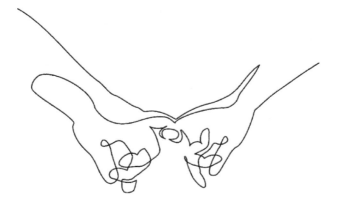

Your masterful
spinning of freshly
polished adverbs
have not yet granted
you entrance to my life.
Each sentence you craft
is an audition
for a part
in my story.
Though I'm starting
to feel the effects
of the way
you whisper
certain
words.

| **Audition**

*Too explosive
to leave unattended,
this chemistry
has rapidly reacted
building an undeniable
but untenable
connection between us.*

| *Reaction*

One
meteoric moment
today of us
throttled all longing
for one hundred
tomorrows
of you.

| **Satiated**

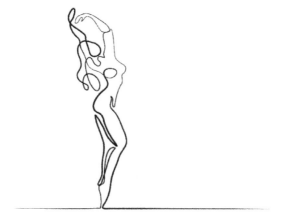

I inhaled the breath
You exhaled
And in a singular moment
We breathed life
Into this
Extraordinary love

| **Kissed to Life**

Ah. Your sun smile.
It's where
my dreams go
to fill up
their ego.

| **Sun Smile**

My life partner,
my soulmate,
you hold me up
when I stumble,
make me
believe
in me
when self-doubt
shows up.
You calm me
when I am anxious
and can't see my way
through to the answer.
Your strength
gives me sustenance.
Through it all
though we have stumbled
we continue to
hold onto,
hold up each other.
You are the haven
I want to run back to
after taking on
the world.

| **Haven**

Lifting each other up
in effortless love
we both
rise higher.

| **When Love Rises**

IN THE DARK

IN THE DARK

I
harbor
this
pain
of
losing
you
in
my
deep
tissue.

| **Deep Tissue**

We were a

Song.

You the melody;

I the lyric.

Now I'm just a note

fallen flat on

your music keys,

when I believed

we'd be a

rousing

symphony.

| **A Song**

What am

I to do

with all of these

Pages of you

that should have been

bound together

into our story?

| **Pages**

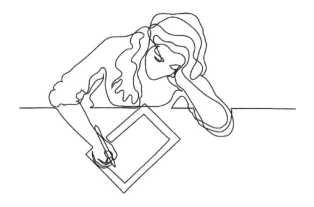

When I hear your voice

My thoughts stumble

Over old memories

And fall off my tongue

Into a tumbled pile

Of puzzled

Words

| **Puzzling**

You found my

indisposed scars

and traced them

back to a bolted shut heart

that endures

despite

multiple break-ins.

I need you to

understand why

the mere promise

of experiencing

your self-declared

exceptional love

is not the magic key

to reopening me.

| **Exposed**

My lips believe
your kisses,
but my heart reads
lie language.

| **Signs**

Seven June's ago today
He promised me
a fresh pearl
to honor each year in-love.
I peer in the mirror
and smooth down
the five white spheres
stranded on my chest,
wondering whether
his promise was
callously forgotten or
just heartlessly
broken.

| **His Promise**

I squeezed
fresh lemons
into old wounds
expecting you
to spread on the honey,
to soothe and sweeten.
You refused
to pour it.

| **Bitters**

With loud
Echoes
Of self-doubt
Rattling
From
Lobe to lobe
My rational mind
Wondered how
I stepped away from
My confident self
Into the lie, that is you.

| **Rattled**

I quietly weep
for our wasted love
as I reach for you
to have and hold.
Once salacious, now
distasteful love,
I touch your hand
and feel only cold.

Never thought
we'd abandon love
once so shiny,
so new, so young.
How'd we break
our promise to love?
The bond that's
supposed to keep us strong.

Our dull and worn
out weary love
leaves a gulf
so wide and deep.
We failed our
precious happy love.
Where's the heart
you gave me to keep?

I cry out loud now
for this wounded love.
No kiss goodnight,
nor warm embrace.
How did I lose
your wanton love,
and the hope in
your angel face?

Yet still, I feel,
though can't find our love,
lost amidst
our deflated dreams.
Ours was sustaining
never-ending love.
But nothing is
ever as it seems.

I'll scream and shout
to retrieve this love.
Won't you stay
with me and fight?
For this wasted,
but still worth it love,
my heart will ache
till we get it right.

| **Wasted**

Yeah,
You just
pretended
to love me
because
it was easier
to lie to me
than to have
your admirers
know the truth
and think less
of you.

| **Narcissist**

And so, it has
come to this,
that our we
no longer exists.
All trust drained
from the sanctity
of these once
heartfelt feelings
because you claim
to have discovered
an emotional tripped wire
resulting in our
faultless connection
gone fatal,
though it was you
who initially
misfired.

| **Fault**

Such pleasure you see
in these dark daily
breakings of me
all to prove
your vaguely veiled
claims of superiority

| *Breaking*

On the night train
I could feel the tracks
reverberate through my body.
Spent with the excitement of
having just experienced
Paris in the twilight,
my meandering mind
kept me from
meeting up with sleep.
I pondered the
days ahead of us
exploring sites in the rain.
Even had I known of the
heart-stopping pain
that lay in wait for me,
I would not turn back
as I could never harness
and hold still
the romancing of
my wanderlust.

| **Wanderlust**

Your betrayal
Deconstructed
All remaining
Bridges
To our
Future.

| **Self-Destruct**

My head says to walk
away from you.
My heart is unprepared
to see it through.
Is it just the distance,
this queasiness in my gut,
or the tiny thread
of a justified distrust
twisting and dividing
it's way between us?

This angst won't end
Can't tell you just why
Even tried to pretend,
turned the other eye.
The empty, the pain,
surely made up in my head.
I know I'll go insane
If I can't put this to bed.
Tell me again the part
where real love holds on.
Can fractured hearts
ever really mend, go on?
Or should I break for it
takeoff, and just run?

| **Just Run**

Our love
took root
and bloomed
in the Spring.
Then your
Winter storm
roared in
scattering me
into the Fall.

| ***Scattered***

That brilliantly
reconstructed
memory we rode here
is now faded and faint
slipping fast away.
Under the cover of night
we made sense.
Come the morning
and its' judging light
gone is the intrigue,
no more suspense.
Listless, we watch
our happy yesteryears
dissipate into
saddened bleak todays.
Though we were never
invited to the celebration
of a future us,
we crashed the party
in reckless style anyway.
Feeling burned.

| **Love Crashers**

I witnessed
all remaining
Love Die
in the
Explosion
behind your
furious glare
before
You
Struck
Me.

| Battered

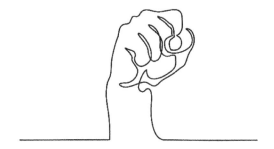

The instant

our eyes locked

I thought that

you were the one

I had sought forever.

So, I forged my way over

never blinking

until our breath

was inches apart,

and our eyes reflected

each other's image.

Abruptly my lips froze.

My words left me

standing there,

abandoned by my senses.

I curved my angst into a smile

and searched your face

for an answer, a future

my date?

In the midst of our moment,

you tore away your eyes

releasing the spell

and scattering my lost words

and our fate

amongst the crowd of

mismatched hearts.

| **Blind Fate**

You spun
those bold
butterfly lies
so impeccably
that I believed
that the alternate
dark life
you cocooned me in
would unfold
into a bright
and beautiful love.
Then I held you
to the light.

| **Butterfly Lies**

My heart is softly breaking
For me there is only you
My soul cries out silently
With every thought of you
My arms are longing
Still yearning
For the tenderness
Of your touch
Your warm embrace
A forehead kiss
That says
You care so much
It isn't right
Can never be fair
That I should feel this way
With you here
So close to me
And yet so far away
My heart is softly breaking
As we bid goodbye today
There is nothing left to give
No words
Remain to say

| **Soft Breaks**

You slipped in,
got under my skin,
then left the scene
without stealing my heart.
Feeling robbed.

| ***Robbed***

I just had to taste
those caramel lies
dripping from
your warm
brown eyes.
Freshly burned,
I'm desensitized
to your sweet kiss,
now hardened,
cold and bittersweet.

| **Caramel Eyes**

I've searched

your many faces

for answers.

Deconstructed your lies.

Tried to reach the real you

in your favorite places.

But you keep pivoting

and twisting

to unsuspecting

hiding spaces.

| **Elusive**

Time

sails

swiftly.

And

eventually

forgets.

It's our

hearts

that

leave us

stranded

in the dark

searching

for a sliver

of

light.

| In The Dark

THE LIGHT

THE LIGHT

Your raging storm
has quieted.
My tears
have receded.
Now I recover the wreckage
you left of my sanity
and commence
my renaissance.

| **My Renaissance**

You were
my favorite word
until the day
I finally forgot
how to spell
you.

| *Dispelled*

Though my
vibrant heart
lay filleted open,
it is incapable
of feeling you
until I've stitched
back together the parts
that are the best of me.
And stirred up a salve
of healing memories
of how love is meant to feel.
Then I shall pluck away
the shards of betrayal
that ripped
my naïve heart
to pieces.
It may take months
or several years,
but first I must
restore me
to me
to make possible
a future us.

| **Restoring Me**

Oh, how my body
remembers
the non-erasable you
that my tortured mind
longs to forget.

| **Torture**

Never diminish

and shrink wrap

your make it happen magic

when he proclaims

intolerance of

your take-charge ways.

Keep flaunting the

fabulously unique you,

that the perfect mate

is certain to find

and soon celebrate.

| **Never Diminish**

I accept

the reality

that Truth

will never meet

You.

| **Stranger to Truth**

No,
nothing
I could ever do
would make you see.
Done bending, mending us
and changing me.

| **Just Done**

Don't want none of yo
reluctant love
Just keep that all to yourself
Need me some of that
free-flowing love
No part of yo
self-absorbed mess

Don't want none of yo
shared kind a love
Ain't enough of you
to go round
No half-stepping here,
no that won't do
Won't be another
jewel in your crown

Don't want no
reluctant love
Put it high up on a shelf
No reluctant love
No reluctant love
Keep it all for yourself

Don't want none of yo
strings attached love
Tell me why I keep
expecting a better you
There's no room
in your heart for me boy
You're too deeply
in love with you

Don't want none of yo
holding back love
Just keep stepping on
along your way
Cause one of these days
I'm gonna find me
Someone I don't
have to entice to stay

Don't want no
reluctant love
That's good for you
but no one else
No reluctant love
No reluctant love
Keep that s#*t to yourself

| **Reluctant Love**

It hurts
where you loved to
rest your head,
so, I no longer sleep
on your favorite
side of the bed.

| *The Middle*

You withheld those
Words for years
dispensing them
like a potion
mixing them in
with my tears
one small drop at a time
until the moment
you learned
I had finally fallen in love
with my own
magnificent story,
the original version of me.
Keep your words.
Open and swallow these.
Good and *bye.*
Please.

| My Words

I'd rather imagine
your innate goodness
than be certain
of your possible
dark intention.

| *Positive Intent*

Why did you

open the door

to your hidden

treasure chest

and let me

make myself at home

only to confess

that my wide open

no limits world

was too broad, fluid,

colorful and intimidating

for your comfortable,

predictable and

controlled life?

| **Too Much for You**

I am done trying on

these different faces.

No more practicing

how to make

excuses

for why you never

show up in

the right places.

| **No More Excuses**

In these
still moments,
alone with my darkness
I have absolute trust that
my lost and estranged
indomitable spirit
will re-emerge
in a fiercer form
and save me
from this
deep disruption
before I am dissolved
into the abyss
of your
disloyal heart.

| **Indomitable**

When he says
I treat you like a queen
You know that you have at once
Been dethroned and belittled
For requiring that you be
Treated with the respect
You deserve
For daring to take the lead
For charging forward
Getting it done
And seeking the most in life
Do not apologize for
The ulterior adulation
He bestowed upon you
Only to tear you down
You owe nothing to no one
Tell him that
You are not his queen
You rule your own kingdom
So, go take
And rock
Your self-made
Crown

| Crowned

Yes, it's done.

You're gone.

Color me sad and blue.

Bristled through the pain,

Cried back the hurt

Of being over with you.

No, we're not us now.

It's just you and just me.

Yes, it's true,

I have bitter feels

But finally,

Love's grip

Has released

Your hold

On me.

| **It's True**

You claim

you were punishing me

by withholding

the best of you.

I never noticed,

so intently focused on

untangling my heart

from the rest of you.

| **Sex Weapon**

Don't invite me into

Your messy life

Then lecture me

Try to school me

On how to

Cleanse my sins

When you only

Come clean

By whitewashing

Your own half-truths

| **Whitewash**

Listen

to my body

when it tells you

that I refuse

to be your reliable host.

| **Dry**

If love
hurts
but you
dutifully stay
and start to lose
the best of you
by slowly slicing away
tiny slivers
of your dignity
with each new day
You must stop
and make a plan
to gather your pieces
to take you back
Yes, decide that today is when
your bags will be packed
so, you can go
retrieve your courage
and make you whole again

| **Whole Again**

Take your time to
visualize a me and a you
while making room for an us
inside of your life.
But know that
But know that I'll be off
designing new life visions
of an in-love
and happy me
with or without
a you.

| *Visualize Me*

Frozen in my steps
I thought I'd lost my mind
Cowered in fear
yet driven by anger
Now newly recovered
I re-imagined my reason
my purpose
and created
a re-entry point where I
reconfigured a happier life
that doesn't include you
Meet the embattled
but stronger
self-loved me

| **Over You**

Here alone,
yet again, just me.
This life lessons'
too slow to come.
We weren't an us,
never meant to be,
Nor I your muse,
your treasured one.
I fell hard,
lived fast in your moment.
now mourn long
for my naïve tears.
Yeah, better choices,
good judgement
would've saved me
all these salty years.

| **Salty Years**

I have at once been angry
disillusioned and inspired
by your reckless life
and disregard for
the sanctity of love.
I refuse to become
a casualty of your
collateral damage.

| **No Collateral**

Why is it that

you were so slow to see

that your disloyalty

inspired me

to take back the key

to my adventurous

wounded heart

opening the door

to "the one"

who made me see

that I am

and will always be

royalty?

| **Royalty**

FROM THE AUTHOR

Thank you for reading my book. I sincerely hope that you enjoyed it and found a connection with some of the poems in a meaningful way. I welcome your reactions and feedback, so please take a moment to leave a rating and review online at the retailer site where you purchased the book.

To stay updated on my next book release, read samples of work in progress, etc., please connect with me as follows:

www.michellestradford.com
Instagram @michellestradfordauthor
Twitter @mgstradford
Facebook @michellestradfordauthor
Pinterest @michellestradfordauthor
Bookbub: michelle-g-stradford
Goodreads: Michelle G. Stradford

ACKNOWLEDGMENTS

First and foremost, I thank God for his many blessings and affording me the opportunity to complete and publish my first book. A heartfelt thanks to my husband for his encouragement, support, and love throughout life and this journey. Thank you to my daughters for filling my life with love and humor and for inspiring me with their fearlessness. To my siblings and extended family, thank you for your unconditional love and encouragement and for being my family jewels. To my treasured friends, I truly value your friendship, authenticity, and love.

ABOUT THE AUTHOR

Michelle G. Stradford is a bestselling Author, Architect, Artist, and Photographer who creates written, visual, and inhabitable art. In addition to poetry, she has written short stories and fiction since adolescence. Her writing style is contemporary free verse, as her goal is to create poetry and prose that is relatable, connects with and is inspiring to her readers. She thrives on using words, art and photography to tell stories that evoke emotions or connects with others and hopes to craft a novel someday. Michelle is married and has two daughters.

Other books by Michelle include **"I'm Rising: Determined. Confident. Powerful."**, the second of three books in her "Rising" series. It is an inspiring poetry collection about self-love written to ignite a spark and remind us that facing and conquering our fears and pain builds inner strength and resilience. **"We All Rise"** is coming soon.